The Great Reform Act
of 1832

LANCASTER PAMPHLETS

The Great Reform Act of 1832

Eric J. Evans

METHUEN · LONDON AND NEW YORK

First published in 1983 by
Methuen & Co. Ltd
11 New Fetter Lane,
London EC4P 4EE

Published in the USA by
Methuen & Co.
in association with Methuen, Inc.
733 Third Avenue, New York,
NY 10017

Typeset in Great Britain by
Scarborough Typesetting Services
and printed by
Richard Clay (The Chaucer Press)
Bungay, Suffolk

British Library Cataloguing in
Publication Data

Evans, Eric J
The great Reform Act of 1832.
 – (Lancaster pamphlets)
1. Great Britain – Parliament
    1830–1837
2. Great Britain – Politics and
    government
3. Great Britain – Constitutional law
    I. Title   II. Series
    328.41   KD3964

ISBN 0–416–34450–X

Contents

Foreword

Lancaster Pamphlets offer concise and up-to-date accounts of major historical topics, primarily for the help of students preparing for Advanced Level examinations, though they should also be of value to those pursuing introductory courses in universities and other institutions of higher education. They do not rely upon prior textbook knowledge. Without being all-embracing, their aims are to bring some of the central themes or problems confronting students and teachers into sharper focus than the textbook writer can hope to do; to provide the reader with some of the results of recent research which the textbook may not embody; and to stimulate thought about the whole interpretation of the topic under discussion. They are written by experienced university scholars who have a strong interest in teaching.

At the end of this pamphlet is a numbered list of the recent or fairly recent works that the writer considers most relevant to his subject. Where a statement or a paragraph is particularly indebted to one or more of these works, the number is given in the text in brackets. This serves at the same time to acknowledge the writer's source and to show the reader where he may find a more detailed exposition of the point concerned.

The Great Reform Act of 1832

Introduction

On 7 June 1832 King William IV gave his royal assent to the first Reform Act. He had many misgivings about the wisdom of the measure and, pointedly, he refused to attend the House of Lords to give the assent in person. He also gave directions that public buildings were not to be illuminated and that no firework display was to be held to mark the event. The Act was passed as the climax to a two-year period of high political tension and excitement both within parliament and outside. Many MPs believed that, unless a measure of parliamentary reform were passed no later than the spring of 1832, a violent revolution would sweep away all established institutions. Chaos and bloodshed, such as the French had experienced forty years earlier during the 'Terror' phase of their revolution, would befall Britain.

The Reform Act was not a piece of timeless constitution-making, the product of a full and dispassionate consideration of the nation's needs. It was a compromise stitched together during a crisis. It dissatisfied a substantial majority of those who had most strenuously urged the need for parliamentary reform. Yet, from the government's point of view, it served its major purpose: it removed the immediate threat to the security of the state. In a broader context, too, the Reform Act deserves to be remembered as one of the most momentous pieces of legislation in the history of modern Britain. As its name implies, it was the first thorough-going attempt to redraw the political map and define which

1

categories of persons should, and which should not, have the vote. No one who studies the later, halting progress towards full parliamentary democracy – the futher extensions of the franchise in 1867, 1884, 1918 and 1928 and the struggle to achieve freedom and, later, equality of votes in 1872, 1883, 1885 and 1948 – can fail to appreciate that 1832 was the vital first step. This was so despite the most deeply rooted convictions of nearly all the MPs who voted for reform in 1832. They believed, with the great historian and Whig politician Thomas Babington Macaulay, that democracy was 'fatal to the purposes for which government exists'. Sir Robert Peel, who opposed the Reform Bill to the very last, but who then proved himself, first as leader of the major opposition party and then as prime minister, one of the best manipulators of the new system, rationalized his objections thus: 'I was unwilling to open a door which I saw no prospect of being able to close.'

The Reform Act, therefore, merits study not only for what it was, but for what it set in motion. Before scrutinizing the Reform Act and its immediate origins, this pamphlet will seek to explain how parliamentary reform came to be the central political issue of the age. Since plans for amending the constitution had been common since at least the 1760s it is also relevant to ask why the reformers had to wait so long to achieve a measure of success. The broader significance of reform will be examined in a final section.

The unreformed parliamentary system

How members came to sit in the House of Commons before 1832 was a haphazard business. Both the qualification to vote in a parliamentary election and the places which had the right to send members to Westminster depended very largely on custom and precedent. Parliamentary seats fell into two broad categories, county and borough; Appendix 3 shows their distribution. Only in the county seats is some uniformity found. Each English county sent two members to parliament, irrespective of its size or population. When elections were contested, the right of voting had since 1430 rested with men who owned freehold land or property to the

2

value of at least forty shillings (£2). They cast two votes for the candidates of their choice in a single election; the *two* candidates with most votes, unlike the modern system, were declared elected. These 'forty shilling freeholders' in England and Wales could be men of very considerable substance or they might own little more than a cabbage patch. This was because the effects of inflation since the fifteenth century had rendered the qualification to vote much easier to achieve than was originally intended. In Scotland, which sent members to the English parliament after the Act of Union in 1707, the right to vote was very much more restricted in both counties and burghs. Only property owners to the value of approximately £100 qualified and most electorates were very small. In 1831, when Scotland's population was 2,364,000 the total electorate was about 4,500. In the county of Bute, which then had a population of 14,000, only 21 electors voted for the two county members.

No attempt was made to link representation to the density of population. This appeared increasingly odd from the late eighteenth century when the industrial revolution was concentrating people in Lancashire, the West Riding of Yorkshire, Staffordshire and Warwickshire. Lancashire's population in 1831 was 1,337,000 yet it sent only two county MPs to Westminster; so did Rutland with a population of 19,000. The majority of English voters, about 55 per cent, voted in county seats despite the fact that only 16 per cent of England's seats were from the counties. The system was extremely hard to justify on rational grounds.

Most, if not all, of England's 203 parliamentary boroughs had been centres of population but some had not thrived since the thirteenth or fourteenth centuries when parliamentary status had been granted. Most had been county towns, market towns or seaports attracting a reasonable degree of commerce. In 1800, a few – Bristol, Coventry, Hull, Liverpool, Plymouth, Preston and, of course, London – remained important centres with rapidly expanding populations. In 1831 London and Liverpool were Britain's two largest cities. A large group, much smaller in population, remained respectable communities with an important range of administrative and mercantile functions. They included county towns like Bedford and Stafford and market towns like Ripon in Yorkshire or Bridgewater in Somerset. Most such communities had populations of 5–10,000.

It was against the third category of parliamentary borough that hostility was directed. These were places which, by the early nineteenth century, were redundant for all purposes but that of providing two MPs. Dunwich in the thirteenth century had been a Suffolk seaport of some note, but coastal erosion had put much of it into the North Sea, leaving 44 houses standing in the borough by 1831. The place had 32 electors for its two members. Old Sarum, two miles to the north of Salisbury, was so derelict that sightseeing tours were arranged to view the ditches and remains of a castle which were all that remained of the old community. Its eleven electors had last been called upon actually to vote in an election in 1715.

None of the Cornish coastal boroughs of Camelford, East Looe and West Looe, Newport, St Germans and St Mawes could muster a population of 1,000 in 1831, but together they placed twelve men in the House of Commons. Three of Surrey's six boroughs – Bletchingley, Haslemere and Gatton – were similarly empty and the last of these had only seven electors.

Thus, sparsely inhabited boroughs sent members to Westminster while many large industrial centres did not. Parliamentary representation entirely failed to keep pace with the shift in the balance of wealth and of population from south to north. In 1831, the cities of Manchester (population 182,000), Birmingham (144,000), Leeds (123,000) and Sheffield (92,000) had not a single MP between them. At the beginning of the nineteenth century, Cornwall with a population of 192,000 sent 44 members to parliament. Lancashire sent a mere fourteen. The southern bias was most notable. In 1801 the six English counties with a southern coastline (including the Isle of Wight) accounted for one third of all England's MPs. (162 out of 489; 150 borough seats, 12 county) through they contained only 15 per cent of her population.

The distribution of seats in parliament was one glaring anomaly in the old system; the right of voting was the other. The wide divergencies in borough voting qualifications were legendary. The system was enormously complex but boroughs may be broadly classified into five types: those in which any adult male who paid local poor rates could vote in an election (the so-called 'scot and lot' boroughs); those in which every resident male of at least six months standing who was not a pauper could vote (the 'potwalloper' boroughs); the 'burgage boroughs' in which voting rights were inherited, virtually as pieces of property; the 'corporation boroughs' in which members of the local corporation were the sole electors; and the 'freeman boroughs' in which the electors were those who qualified in various ways to be considered freemen. Most of the electorates in the first two categories were wide in late-eighteenth-century terms, with more than 500 voters per borough. The third and fourth categories were very small, with electorates usually less than 100. In the fifth category, since the definition of freeman could be interpreted widely or narrowly, both large and small electorates were found.

Defenders of the old system made a virtue of this diversity, arguing that it ensured the representation of a wide, though unequal, range of interests. They also argued that, since property rather than numbers had traditionally been the appropriate qualification for electoral representation, statistics about population growth in electorally under-represented areas were irrelevant. Diversity certainly produced interesting effects. The seven biggest borough electorates – Bristol, Leicester, London, Liverpool, Nottingham, Preston and Westminster – were larger than 5,000. Some approached universal male suffrage, which no post-1832 borough did. Here, as in more populous county constituencies like Middlesex, elections in the eighteenth and early nineteenth centuries could be real tests of public opinion. Overwhelmingly, however, the right to vote in the boroughs was vested in small, unrepresentative minorities. In 1830, 43 of the 202 English boroughs had electorates in excess of 1,000 but 113 had fewer than 300 and 56 of these were truly 'rotten boroughs' with fewer than 50 voters each. A parliamentary reform organization in 1780 calculated that the total electorate of England and Wales was about 214,000 when the total population was approaching 8 million.

The British system of government had actually become less representative in the course of the eighteenth century. First, the electorate of England and Wales in 1715 was about 260,000. By 1832, according to Professor Cannon's recent estimate (1), it had risen (mostly because of extra voters in the counties and the biggest boroughs) by about 32 per cent to 344,000. Since population rose in the same period by about 155 per cent (approximately $5\frac{1}{2}$ million to 14 million) the conclusion on representation is obvious.

Second, and probably more important, the opportunities for that electorate to vote were dwindling. During the reign of Queen Anne (1702–14) elections had to be held every three years and the elections between Whig and Tory were furiously contested. After the Whigs had established overwhelming political dominance in 1715, general elections became far less contentious. After 1734, no general election before 1832 in England saw more than 11 county contests or more than 82 borough ones. In 1761 only four English counties and forty-two boroughs were actually contested. Members for all other seats were returned unopposed. Not only had the Whigs hastened to increase the maximum length of parliament from three years to seven by the 1716 Septennial Act, when elections did come round they were low key affairs. They almost never brought a change of government and rarely raised important issues.

The reason for all of this, in one word, was patronage. Patronage was the keystone of unreformed British politics. Elections became unnecessary because constituencies were effectively the property of great landlords or of the crown. The voters might be tenants of the borough 'proprietor' or they might have financial or other inducements not to vote for any candidate other than the proprietor's nominee. An election, therefore, was a waste of time. No one would challenge a candidate nominated by Earl Fitzwilliam for the Northamptonshire borough of Higham Ferrers, for example, and no election was held there between 1702 and the borough's abolition in 1832. The two seats for Appleby (Cumbria) were shared between the Earls of Lonsdale and Thanet. Sir Philip Francis gave an amusing account of his selection there in 1802: 'I was unanimously elected by one elector to represent this ancient borough in Parliament . . . there was no other candidate, no Opposition, no Poll demanded. . . . So I had nothing to do but

6

to thank the said elector for the Unanimous Voice with which I was chosen. . . . On Friday morning I shall quit this triumphant Scene with flying Colours and a noble determination not to see it again in less than seven years'.

Roughly half of Britain's MPs sat in Westminster because a patron had put them there. Since voting was an open declaration of allegiance and not a secret ballot, landowners could easily check whether electors defied them. It is not surprising that about one-fifth of all MPs were the sons of peers; their fathers feathered the family nest. Nor is it surprising that fewer than one third of parliamentary seats were contested in the century before the Reform Act.

Even the avoidance of elections, however, was expensive. Borough patrons had to consider the material comforts of 'their' electors. 'Keeping up the interest' could cost a nobleman upwards of £5,000 during the course of a parliament. The Grosvenor family was alleged to spend £4,000 a year in the late eighteenth century to ensure continued control of the borough of Chester. Nearly all borough 'owners' were great landowners, though successful businessmen could buy their way to political influence via a seat in parliament. The price − between £4,000 and £6,000 at the turn of the century − deterred all but the most wealthy. Nevertheless, Bedford became the preserve of the Whitbread brewing family; Tamworth, in Staffordshire, was shared between the Marquis of Townshend and Sir Robert Peel senior, the cotton magnate from Bury, who used the borough to launch the political careers of his sons William and the future prime minister, Robert junior.

Influence did not prevent the occasional contest. Bedford and Tamworth were both contested once between 1800 and 1832 and elections could be dreadfully expensive. In smaller boroughs electors would not vote unless they were handsomely 'treated' and in the larger boroughs bribery was so common as to be endemic. Stories circulated of specific contests, such as the Lincoln by-election of 1808, costing upwards of £25,000 and of families being ruined by contests in which they overmatched. Even an ordinary election could cost several thousand pounds, not just in bribes, but in travelling expenses. Many borough voters in

Cornish seats required transport from London to cast their votes (there was no postal ballot). They would expect appropriate accommodation while away and adequate recompense to induce them, however temporarily, to quit the pleasures of the capital for some remote Celtic wilderness. Only one polling station was available in a county election and travelling expenses for a large electorate to visit the county town were steep.

The poll itself, as the work of the artist Hogarth reminds us, was a boisterous if not a riotous affair. Affrays were frequent; the antics of rival groups of frequently intoxicated supporters brings vividly to mind the weekly romps of contending partisans in a more modern spectator sport. For the voters, and often for the town as a whole, an election was an event to be savoured. Not only did the candidates provide free beer, but a poll which lasted a couple of weeks to allow distant voters travelling time kept the drink flowing. Since open voting was practised, the drama of the contest was heightened. Candidates could check running totals and know which palms had yet to be greased, which absent voters cajoled to the poll. The whole business was pure, or perhaps more accurately impure, theatre.

Why did pressure for parliamentary reform grow?

Criticism of the unreformed system grew markedly in the second half of the eighteenth century. Those who desired change fell into two categories. Firstly, there were those, mainly from the propertied classes with access to influential friends if not influential themselves, who wished to eliminate the worst features of the old system, but they envisaged control of government remaining firmly in the hands of men of property and education. Secondly, there were those, mostly without much property, who saw participation in the choosing of a nation's rulers as an essential right of all its citizens, regardless of wealth. Sadly, few would have categorized women as citizens. For all but a very tiny minority the demand for 'universal male adult suffrage' meant precisely that.

The parliamentary reform movement grew for three main reasons. Within parliament and, more especially among voters in

8

county constituencies, disquiet was growing at the way in which influence or patronage determined matters at Westminster. It seemed particularly objectionable that an ineffective and unpopular government could keep itself in office by putting pressure on those members representing rotten boroughs controlled by government supporters (including the crown) to vote solidly for it. Lord North's ministry (1770–82) was prolonged at least three years by George III's determination to uphold it by the exercise of royal patronage, even against the judgment of a prime minister who was anxious to quit. Many country gentlemen thought it monstrous that a government responsible for the disasters of the American War of Independence and the loss of the American colonies should thus be kept in office. Their representatives in the Commons, the English county MPs, normally supported the government of the day, but after 1777, when the battle of Saratoga was lost, they began to desert it. Yet North survived even this. The numerical under-representation of the county MPs was forcibly impressed upon them, which was the more galling since county members were in general the most independent-minded and least corruptible in the House. Not surprisingly, one of the earliest reform movements, that founded in Yorkshire in 1779 by the Rev. Christopher Wyvill, called for increased county representation and for various checks on the government, the most notable of which was the need to fight elections more frequently. Its members, overwhelmingly, were landowners – Wyvill himself was a landowning Anglican clergyman – and its target the corruption of the executive.

The second spur to parliamentary reform was economic change. The under-representation of Britain's leading commercial and industrial centres (see pp. 3–4) became the more difficult to justify with every year that passed. Some unofficial arrangements had been made, but these were not enough. After 1774, Birmingham manufacturers exercised influence in the nomination for one of the two Warwickshire county seats which partially compensated for the town's non-representation. The business community of Southwark, in south London, secured the return of a radical MP, Sir Joseph Mawbey, for the county seat of Surrey in the 1770s, much to the disgust of many country gentlemen. The growing needs of industry, however, were obvious and many parliamentary reformers whose main concern was an increase in county membership felt it prudent to link that demand with one for separate representation of the major towns.

The third reason was ideological and, ultimately, the most powerful. In the second half of the eighteenth century European writers and philosophers, particularly in France, were redefining the relationship between the individual and the state. This was one aspect of the so-called European Enlightenment. Most of its advocates believed that the authority of governments over their subjects ultimately rested upon an implicit contract between governors and governed, whereby the governed gave up certain rights of independent action and initiative to the governors in return for benefits which only a government could bestow, such as security and a framework of laws to protect society from internal and external enemies. From this line of reasoning, it followed that ordinary men possessed basic rights which no government could take away. Jean-Jacques Rousseau's book, *Du Contrat Social*, published in 1762, argued that any contract between governors and governed rested on the right of each citizen to participate in the choosing of his governors. Democracy, therefore, was the only legitimate basis for the exercise of authority by any government. The ideas of Rousseau and other Enlightenment thinkers directly challenged the despots who ruled most European states, but they also came to have a profound impact in Britain, which was certainly not an autocracy, but which was equally far from being a democracy. Britain was a type of oligarchy since power was exercised by a subtle blend of monarchy with limited, but not negligible, powers and a parliament controlled by wealthy landowners.

For those who sympathized with the Enlightenment, Britain's hybrid government was scarcely less objectionable than a despotism. When the French Revolution broke out in 1789 it was seen as a supreme vindication of the new thinking and the parliamentary reform movement gained immensely by its example. After 1789, British writers and intellectuals from the middle ranks of society had much more success in carrying their message down the social scale, at least as far as the skilled working men in cities

10

like London, Sheffield and Norwich which had a high proportion of craftsmen who were both literate and politically aware. The book which became the bible of such men, Tom Paine's _The Rights of Man_, appeared in two parts in 1791–2; it rapidly became one of the eighteenth century's best-sellers. It stated universal manhood suffrage to be the only legitimate basis for government; it anticipated and even prophesied the imminent collapse of all European monarchies, including the British; it advocated disarmament, since democracies would never need to make war on one another; it proposed swingeing, confiscatory taxes on all inherited wealth, a hereditary landowner appearing to Paine as an absurd concept. With the money saved on defence and collected in taxes, Tom Paine's democracy would establish free, compulsory education, pensions, family allowances and a range of welfare benefits most of which were not to be widely available in Britain until after 1945.

Paine's work owed everything to the European Enlightenment. It was essentially a supreme work of propaganda. It simplified complex concepts in language which a wider audience could understand; it was racily written and well spiced with telling epigrams. It appealed directly to an audience of working people anxious for advancement and susceptible to the cruel oversimplification that all their hardships derived from the illegitimate exercise of power by government. Legitimate authority, they learned, could be given only by the governed and the vast majority of the governed never had an opportunity to bestow it in a free election.

The French Revolution was a watershed in the history of parliamentary reform. Before it, pressure came primarily from the middle and even the upper ranks. After 1789, though these groups were by no means eclipsed, the reform movement was increasingly influenced by democrats who sought a government with a much broader social base, and regularly elected by universal male suffrage. As the industrial revolution concentrated ever more people in the towns of south-east Lancashire, the West Riding of Yorkshire and the central valley of Scotland, so the arguments for such a government grew. How could a parliament of landowners, representing places like Dunwich or West Looe, possibly know how to govern cotton spinners from Bolton or weavers from Paisley?

Parliamentary reformers, 1789–1820

The campaign to secure a reform of parliament did not begin with the French Revolution. The activities of parliamentary reformers before 1789 must be traced elsewhere (1, 3, 4). Suffice it to say that they mostly reflected middle class, and particularly country gentlemen's, fears about the control of government by means of influence and corruption. Reform was necessary as a purifying agent. Reformers had been strongest in London where the main pressure group had been the Society for Constitutional Information (SCI), and in Yorkshire.

Reform, however, was revived and extended as an issue by events in France. The overthrow of Europe's most powerful autocracy and its replacement by a National Assembly allegedly favouring those noble, if amorphous, ideals of liberty, equality and fraternity inspired reformers everywhere. In Britain the chairman of the Society for Constitutional Information, the MP Henry Flood, raised the reform issue in the Commons in March 1790. Avoiding the impression that he was a wild revolutionary he advocated a widening of the franchise to include householders, but stopped well short of universal male suffrage. 'Numbers', he dutifully told the House, 'are necessary to the spirit of liberty.' But he recognized that property must continue to exercise the decisive influence because property was 'conducive to the spirit of order'. He also indicated that he favoured reform precisely because he was 'no friend to revolutions . . . I am, therefore, a friend to timely reform, and for this reason, that it renders revolutions unnecessary.'

Flood's motion did not reach a vote, but his speech is important in indicating a line of reasoning much favoured by middle-class and aristocratic reformers right up to 1832. Most wished to preserve a government rooted in property rather than 'mere numbers'; not to reform, however, would be the most dangerous course of all. Men without hope of change or concession from their governors would look to bloody revolution. Particularly once the French Revolution moved into its 'terror' phase from 1792, with Jacobins in control, the French king and queen executed and what appeared to alarmed observers in Britain to be a wholesale march of the aristocracy to the guillotine, the argument of 'reform in order to preserve' gained strength. Even so, the majority view in parliament remained that the best way to guard against revolution in Britain was to stamp early and firmly on any manifestation of support for 'French principles'.

Outside parliament, the SCI produced large numbers of pamphlets in favour of reform, many of them advocating democracy. By May 1792 the society was even sending letters of encouragement to the Jacobin club in Paris, assuring it of steadily increasing support in Britain. John Horne Tooke, an active radical since the 1760s, and other SCI leaders were making contact with working men, educating them in political organization and urging them to establish their own societies. The results were spectacular. A Constitutional Society was founded in Sheffield late in 1791 and over the next two years a string of radical societies of working men were founded in most of Britain's larger towns. Most took both their name and their lead from the London Corresponding Society (LCS), founded in January 1792 by a Scottish shoemaker, Thomas Hardy, with active assistance from Tooke. As the names of these societies indicate, they spread reform doctrines throughout the country by correspondence and other expressions of mutual support. Meetings were held in local public houses; constitutions of extraordinary precision were drawn up; tracts and pamphlets were published; the French were bombarded with messages of support. Their intellectual inspiration was Tom Paine (see p. 11) and their commitment to one man, one vote followed the arguments in *The Rights of Man*. Corresponding society members bought huge numbers of copies of the cheap editions of a book whose arguments formed the basis of many a public house discussion.

In fostering working men's political societies, was the SCI nursing a viper at its bosom? On one interpretation, the mobilization of working-class support was necessary to mount the kind of pressure for reform which the government could not ignore. But after 1792 parliamentary reform could never again be restricted to polite discussion among articulate intellectuals, lawyers and manufacturers. Many artisans who joined the corresponding societies did so because their trade was depressed and their wage levels threatened. They looked to political reform to improve their economic position. Few working men could afford the luxury of dispassionate appeals to reason. For them, democracy offered a more potent weapon in the struggle for existence.

Not all of this was clear to those members of the SCI, and there were many, who distrusted democracy. Horne Tooke was a case in point: he was a radical and a libertarian, but no democrat. He assisted working-class radical societies in 1791 and 1792 because he believed in their power to strengthen the pressure for reform, but he could hardly applaud when they hastened to pass resolutions in favour of universal manhood suffrage and the abolition of both monarchy and the House of Lords. Nor, as a beneficed clergyman, did he approve the tendency in many societies towards freethought and atheism. He had helped to unleash a force which he could not control.

At the beginning of their brief career, the corresponding societies had believed that their objectives could be achieved by organization and the petitioning of parliament. In this delusion they were encouraged partly by the writings of Paine, which conveyed the naïve impression that issues were decided on the basis of strength of argument, and partly by a new organization of aristocratic Whig politicians, the Association of the Friends of the People, founded in April 1792. This exclusive club, with the prohibitively high annual subscription of $2\frac{1}{2}$ guineas, attracted young reformers like Charles Grey, Thomas Erskine and Richard Brinsley Sheridan, the playwright. Its members were contemptuous of the fears of their more senior political friends, who were now rapidly turning against reform, but they were also anxious to control the direction of radical agitation. Most of them feared democracy as much as the most fervent anti-reformers, but they calculated that the best way of avoiding it was to 'adopt' the radical societies and channel their enthusiasms in a safe direction. For a time, they succeeded. The Friends of the People helped to orchestrate a petitioning campaign which led to a debate in the Commons on the principle of reform in May 1793. By that time, however, Louis XVI had been executed by the French revolutionaries, Britain was at war with France and parliamentary opinion had never been so hostile to reform. The motion was lost by 282 votes to 41.

Extra-parliamentary reformers now struggled in an intensely unfavourable climate. Scottish reformers, encouraged by two conventions in 1792 and early 1793, invited the English radical societies to send representatives to a national convention in Edinburgh in November and December 1793. The very title, taken directly from France, alarmed the authorities. Some radicals were indeed toying with the idea of declaring that they, rather than an unrepresentative parliament, were the true leaders of the people, since parliament had so contemptuously rejected their petitions. The authorities now felt ready to move, and the London Corresponding Society delegates, Maurice Margarot and Joseph Gerrald, were arrested together with the Scottish secretary of the convention, William Skirving, charged with sedition, and sentenced to transportation for fourteen years (5, 6).

Increasingly secure of the support of propertied opinion, the government now mounted a direct attack on the radicals. The suspension of Habeas Corpus in May 1794 enabled political suspects to be held indefinitely without trial. A dozen leading reformers from the SCI and the LCS were arrested on charges of treason, and although a London jury refused to convict the three, including Hardy and Tooke, who were eventually brought to trial, the episode frightened many reformers. Neither Hardy nor Tooke played a significant role in radical leadership again; Tooke even allowed himself to be selected for parliament in 1801 for the rotten borough of Old Sarum under the patronage of the Earl of Caledon. Once the government had bared its teeth, propertied reformers from the Friends of the People and the SCI showed every sign of fearing the bite. They also responded in some measure to patriotic rallying cries during the war. Though both groups helped the corresponding societies to mount impressive public demonstrations against the Seditious Meetings and Treasonable Practices Acts which the government rushed through parliament during the economic depression at the end of 1795 and which significantly curtailed both meetings and political debate,

15

the government's policy against the radicals succeeded almost totally. The LCS, which had a membership of 5,000 at its peak and at least as many active sympathizers, became after 1795 a small, isolated group, deprived of its normal channels of communication by the 'Two Acts' and dominated in its final years by revolutionaries seeking an alliance with Irish republicans and the French to bring the government down by force. Its last public meeting, in St Pancras in July 1797, was declared illegal and dispersed by the magistrates. By the time Pitt formally banned the LCS in 1799 it had totally lost its old power to bring crowds onto the streets and it had almost no middle-class allies.

Grey, meanwhile, made a final effort. He produced an old plan drawn up by the Whig Friends of the People and presented it to parliament as a Reform Bill in May 1797. He deliberately chose a time when the war was going badly; economic discontent was manifest and the government was forced to raise taxes. There seemed every prospect of independent support, as in 1780–2. The circumstances of 1797, however, were entirely different. Fear of France was now paramount and Grey's proposals to give a vote to every householder and to increase county representation by about 20 seats were defeated by 256 votes to 91.

From 1797 to 1815, when the French wars finally ended, the reform question was generally in the background, but the period is not without importance. High food prices and widespread unemployment brought pro-reform crowds onto the streets of the new Lancashire cotton towns in 1797 and 1801. A growing political awareness in the industrial areas was to be an important factor in the later phases of the reform campaign. At the general election of 1802 reformers could take at least two crumbs of comfort from results in the larger constituencies: Sir Francis Burdett, a wealthy radical, was elected at Middlesex while in Norwich the arch anti-reformer, William Windham, was defeated by a non-conformist reformer, William Smith.

The reformers' main problem in keeping the pot boiling was the lukewarmness of the Whig opposition. Reformers were a minority in the Whig party and when Samuel Whitbread, one of their leaders, began attending reform meetings in London in 1809 he was bitterly criticized by his colleagues, including Grey whose passions had notably cooled since 1797. In their turn the radicals poured scorn on a venture sponsored by the Whigs which did achieve success. In 1809 the Whig MP John Christian Curwen got a Bribery Act onto the statute book. It prescribed fines and disqualification for any member of parliament who offered inducements to vote. But no one tried hard to make the act work and bribery continued as before. Burdett's proposal to enfranchise householders was overwhelmingly defeated in the same year and in 1810 a better prepared case by Thomas Brand for a similar franchise extension and the reduction of parliament's maximum life to three years was defeated by 234 to 115. Brand's motion represented progress. No reform proposal had received more than 100 votes in the Commons since Pitt's in 1785.

The renewed impetus for reform, however, came from outside parliament. In the last years of the war economic warfare between Britain and France almost stifled Britain's overseas markets, resulting in widespread unemployment and rocketing food prices. The consequent distress offered fertile soil for the radical message of reformers such as Major John Cartwright who made a tour of the midlands and northern industrial areas to spread the gospel of reform based on collaboration between the middle and working classes. In 1812 a group of prosperous London-based radicals, led by Cartwright and Burdett (now MP for Westminster) had formed a Hampden Club, named after one of the foremost opponents of Charles I's personal rule in the 1630s, to agitate for a franchise of taxpayers.

Cartwright succeeded in stimulating reform activity in the north, but the results were not what he anticipated. Peace returned in 1815 accompanied by further economic distress and the main manufacturing areas began to organize radical movements of their own. These showed a healthy aversion to following the lead of middle-class and aristocratic reform associations. The provincial Hampden Clubs, particularly numerous in the weaving villages of south Lancashire, called for full manhood suffrage and they organized a massive petitioning campaign in 1816–17. The 1817 parliamentary session received over 700 petitions from 350 towns, mostly from the manufacturing areas of the Midlands, Lancashire, Yorkshire and central Scotland. The London radicals also arranged huge political meetings at which the tub-thumping oratory of yet another middle-class reformer, Henry ('Orator') Hunt, made a great impression.

The revival of reform between 1812 and 1817 is noteworthy in several respects: it was on a much broader scale than anything seen before, but, more significantly, it was no longer directed from London. Though the capital remained important, the focus of attention had shifted northwards to precisely those areas where political representation was most flimsy and where the growth of population and manufacturing industry most suggested the need for change. The growth of political awareness both in large factories and small workshops was most marked. The circulation of radical newspapers, led by the weekly *Cobbett's Political Register* but ably and wittily supported by Thomas Wooler's *Black Dwarf* and William Sherwin's *Political Register* was unprecedentedly large. By 1820 government publications were outnumbered, out-written and out-argued by pro-reform material.

This movement also involved an alliance between the middle and working classes to extract reform from an aristocratic parliament. This was new, but it now became a critical factor in reform agitation. Working men were now better able to argue their own case and no longer needed the teacher-pupil relationship which had existed between the SCI and the LCS in 1792. Similarly, a separate manufacturers' political interest was much more noticeable after the economic confusion of the last years of the war. Perhaps the greatest factor in this alliance was a new Corn Law, which parliament passed in 1815. This restricted the import of foreign corn into Britain; its primary purpose was to keep domestic prices high in the interests of farmers and landowners. It was denounced as 'class' legislation, and manufacturers argued that landowners were feathering their own nests. Not only were industrialists denied similar protective legislation, but, since the Corn Law kept food prices high, it was reducing the amount of cash available for workers to buy manufactured goods. Working men argued that protection for those whose interests were fully represented in parliament meant crippling prices for the basic necessity of life for the rest of the community. The new Corn Law provided perfect ammunition to attack the unreformed political system.

The Reform agitation of 1815–20 took several forms. In addition to a ceaseless propaganda blast in the reform press, an attempted armed march by weavers from Manchester to London in 1817 was broken up by the yeomanry at Stockport. This was called the 'March of the Blanketeers' from the covering which the demonstrators took with them on their projected long journey. An actual rebellion in Derbyshire (The Pentridge Rising) the same year was foiled and its leaders executed. In the summer of 1819, during a severe trade recession, four massive political rallies were held in large cities. At the last of these, in St Peter's Fields, Manchester in August, the local yeomanry forcibly dispersed the crowds by a sabre charge, killing eleven people in the process. These victims of the 'Peterloo Massacre' (a name coined in ironic reference to the Battle of Waterloo) became the most celebrated martyrs in the cause of parliamentary reform. In 1820 a group of reformers who wished to go so far beyond mere reform as to abolish the aristocracy and share out the land almost as peasant communes, planned to blow up the Cabinet and take power by *coup d'etat*. This 'Cato Street Conspiracy' was easily foiled by the government's intelligence network and the leading conspirator, Arthur Thistlewood, was hanged at Newgate with four of his accomplices.

Outwardly, at least, the government of Lord Liverpool, which lasted from 1812 to 1827, remained inflexible, meeting the challenge with weapons similar to those employed by the younger Pitt in the 1790s. Habeas Corpus was again suspended in 1817 and magistrates were given additional powers to control public meetings. After the Peterloo affair, the government passed Six Acts to quell popular agitation. These concentrated on controlling public meetings and subjecting radical newspapers to punitive taxation to raise their price and, it was hoped, restrict their circulation and influence.

Why were the earlier reformers unsuccessful?

Given the amount of radical agitation in the two generations before the Reform Act, it seems sensible to ask why parliamentary reform was delayed until 1832. Ironically the very event which gave reformers most encouragement, the French Revolution, also made the passage of a reform bill through parliament much less likely.

This irony is easily unravelled. Before 1789, reform was a respectable topic for polite debate. Few disagreed that the old system was capricious and haphazard, or denied that the rise of new economic forces strengthened the case for constitutional change. Few wished to see Manchester or Birmingham permanently without direct representatives. Yet equally few in parliament would accept a reform which changed the very nature of the British constitution. Thus when changes were discussed, they were envisaged as growing naturally out of a system whose glory (so its defenders asserted) was its flexibility and diversity (see p. 5).

The change which came about after 1789 was precisely the change in established opinion which converted Pitt the Younger from a reformer to a firm political conservative. The French Revolution had inspired the politically unrepresented throughout Western Europe but it thoroughly alarmed a generation of aristocrats. Reformers became tarred with the undiscriminating brush of revolution and any attempt to disturb Britain's precisely poised constitution could be interpreted as pushing it towards the wildest of Jacobin excesses. As early as 1790, during Flood's reform motion (see p. 12) William Windham was making a point which would be flung incessantly at that dwindling band of MPs who favoured change: 'Would he [Flood] recommend you to repair your house in the hurricane season?' Virtually the whole of Pitt's speech against Grey's reform proposals in 1793 was a tirade against the 'excesses and outrages' associated with 'French principles'. All reformers were guilty by association. Pitt, as an old reformer, was careful to absolve himself. He would, he said, 'rather forego for ever the advantages of reform, than risk for a moment the existence of the British constitution'.

The widening of the reformers' social base further weakened their attractiveness in Parliament. What the reformers *were* was at least as important as what they said. The artisans and other working men of the corresponding societies in the 1790s bore an

20

unacceptable resemblance to the Jacobin *sans culottes* and petty traders of Paris. Even had this parallel not been available, it is unlikely that a parliament of educated, privileged men would willingly have conceded the kind of franchise reforms which would see members elected by men who were so much their social inferiors. The existing political system might be irrational, but it did guarantee a legislature dominated by men of property, education and pedigree; to these men universal manhood suffrage was a recipe for ignorance and chaos. Men like Sheridan and Grey who advocated the kind of reforms which Pitt and many others still in parliament had supported ten years earlier were now dismissed as dupes. In the revolution which would follow reform, Pitt argued, democrats would push propertied reformers aside just as surely as they pushed the anti-reformers.

Had the French Revolution not intervened, it is most likely that a modest measure of parliamentary reform, certainly including an extension of county and large-borough representation and probably also some rationalization of the voting qualification would have been passed in the 1790s, and William Pitt the Younger might well have been its sponsor. The Revolution also cast a long shadow. Not only were reform prospects blighted in the 1790s but memories of 1789 were to counsel caution in the next generation. Pitt died in 1806, but those who had come to prominence under him – Liverpool, Castlereagh and Canning – remained hostile to reform into the 1820s for much the same reasons as Pitt himself. George Canning provides a good example of this reasoning. He is known to students primarily for his 'liberal' foreign policy, for fostering nations in South America struggling to break free from the old Spanish and Portuguese colonial empires. He also strongly supported removing political disabilities from Roman Catholics. He was not by any stretch of the imagination a general opponent of change. Yet on the question of parliamentary reform he never wavered. He had first come to prominence in 1797 as editor of the *Anti-Jacobin*, a periodical produced to stiffen the resolve of the propertied classes against the follies and dangers of reform. In another age, he might have mellowed into a moderate reformer, but the French Revolution was no ordinary political upheaval. It convinced a generation of

21

political leaders that the fight against parliamentary reform was a crusade for civilization.

Though many were slow to recognise it, parliamentary reformers had eventually to admit that their cause would not be won swiftly or by power of argument alone. In this, Tom Paine was quite wrong. Parliament would legislate for its own reform only under threat. The most potent threat, obviously, was fear of what might happen if parliament remained intransigent. In the 1790s, working-class support was only just beginning to be mobilized across the nation and middle-class or aristocratic reformers were easily frightened or isolated by anti-reform legislation. Sustained, concerted pressure could not be mounted on the government. Between 1812 and 1820 the reformers' strength outside parliament grew enormously. The alliance between the middle and working classes, however, (pp. 16–19), was still too new and too fragile to frighten parliament into submission and it was all too likely to be disturbed by conflict between manufacturer and workforce over rates of pay or conditions of work. In parliament, determination to resist reform remained strong while memories of the French Revolution remained fresh. Radical Whigs, like Brougham, Burdett or Romilly, had the greatest difficulty in persuading their leadership that Reform was a worthwhile cause for an opposition to espouse. Votes on reform in 1812, 1817 and 1818 show deep Whig divisions on the issue. But the changing mood of the country eventually had its effect at Westminster. By 1820 Sir Robert Peel was asking a close political colleague:

Do not you think that the tone of England . . . is more liberal . . . than the policy of the government? Public opinion never had such influence on public measures, and yet never was so dissatisfied with the share it possessed. It is growing too large for the channels it has been accustomed to run through. . . . Can we resist for seven years [the length of a parliament] reform in Parliament?

The Reform Act crisis 1827–32

No serious possibility of reform had existed before 1827. The economy had been generally buoyant in the early 1820s and employment prospects bright: inevitably popular agitation had waned. Yet, with its waning, it had become safer for MPs individually to declare their support for change in the electoral system. With the middle classes apparently in favour of reform, and with no working-class crowds agitating in the streets, the Whig leadership had begun to see the political advantages of raising the issue again. Lord John Russell introduced a bill in 1822 to remove one of the two members for the smallest boroughs and to transfer their representation to the counties and largest towns. Though defeated by 269 votes to 164, Russell achieved the biggest pro-Reform vote since 1785. A similar bill in the next session, however, received less support and reformers had to be content with a solitary, token, success. After immense haggling a bill was passed in 1821 to disfranchise the Cornish borough of Grampound on grounds of corruption and to transfer its two seats to the biggest county, Yorkshire. The disfranchisement came into effect with the election of 1826 but, characteristically, the Yorkshire county seat was uncontested in that year, so the change did not increase electoral choice. Grampound was unimportant in itself, but this minor step at least breached the ultra-purist anti-reform argument that the sacred constitution was inviolable. If parliament could disfranchise one borough, it could dispense with a hundred on a simple vote.

The reformers' tide ebbed once more; the question hardly figured in the 1826 election. At the beginning of 1827, Lord Liverpool remained in total control of a Tory government more in agreement about the undesirability of changing the constitution than on any other issue. But, paralysed by a stroke, Liverpool resigned in February. Within a year, party politics were in total disarray and from the resulting confusion the reformers profited. Liverpool's value to the Tories was never so apparent as in the few months after his resignation. His supreme talent lay in his ability to get naturally more gifted subordinates to work in harmony under him. Without him, the Tories squabbled and split, partly because of vanity and envy (attributes not to be under-estimated in politics, where personality is at least as important as policy) partly on specific issues.

Liverpool's successor was Canning, a brilliant man whose

talent for biting sarcasm and manifest intolerance of mediocrity made him many permanent enemies. He was also distrusted among the 'protestants' from Liverpool's Cabinet for supporting Roman Catholic emancipation (see p. 26). For men like the Duke of Wellington, Lord Eldon and Robert Peel (whose ten-year period as Chief Secretary for Ireland had not softened his heart towards Catholics) the supremacy of the Anglican church was a central pillar of the established order. Allowing Catholics to sit in parliament would weaken that pillar. These three refused to serve Canning and were replaced by the Whig politicians, Tierney, Lansdowne and Carlisle, much to the annoyance of Grey and the rest of the Whig leadership. Canning's brief premiership thus split both parties. When he died after a few months he was replaced by Viscount Goderich who proved a hopelessly weak leader.

After Goderich's resignation, the Duke of Wellington was asked in January 1828 to form a government. Wellington's generally conservative views were well known and it was assumed that his term of office would greatly strengthen the anti-reformers. In fact, his ministry, which lasted almost three years, progressively demoralized them and when it fell in November 1830 it was replaced by a Whig government pledged to reform.

The explanation for this rapid change of fortunes is only partly political, but Wellington's ineptitude as a politician needs stressing. Wellington himself would probably have denied that he was a politician at all; he expressed contempt for political squabbles and petty office-seeking. But aristocratic disdain allied to soldierly commonsense were not appropriate equipment for the complex tasks which lay ahead. When events began to move rapidly, Wellington was usually behind the game. In particular, he behaved as if opposition was of no account, especially when it surfaced within his government. He had included Liberal Tories, inheritors of the Canning tradition, only reluctantly and he removed them as soon as opportunity offered. Canning's old friends, now led by William Huskisson, had not retained his specific aversion to parliamentary reform and in 1828 they supported Lord John Russell's proposal from the Whig benches to disfranchise two more corrupt boroughs – Penryn (Cornwall)

rope. The July Revolution was an
 of 1789.
me to draw breath, agricultural
 and demoralized by harvest failures
egun to burn hayricks in a series of
) which continued from August 1830
ndowners feared that if agricultural
 docile and least politically conscious
 into their own hands then the entire
The problem now was that, wherea
19, MPs had rightly believed that law
d by a series of repressive statutes and
n trials, evidence was now mounting
30–1 might spark off a full scale rebel
 seriously to contemplate concessions
mentary reform the only way to avoi

ystem provided evidence in 1830 of th
 Westminster. The death of George
al election, which perceptibly weakene
. It was not that the election destroye
unreformed elections were not like tha
lace to make a total change in politic
government influence in many Corni
d remained strong. Yet, traditionall
engthened the government's hand. T
that of 1784, had given the new prin
entary majority which he had previous
oked similarly to the 1830 election
t he was sorely disappointed. An attem
he Canning-Huskisson wing of the To
Party managers ruefully recognized th
no longer carried its old weight. Notab
, such as John Wilson Croker and Pee
defeated. Where contests were held in t
hose brave enough to declare themselves
resoundingly beaten. Long standing an
mas Gooch, a Suffolk MP since 1806 a

and East Retford (Nottinghamshire) and to reallocate their seats to Manchester and Birmingham. When Peel proposed a government amendment which would have given the East Retford seats not to a large manufacturing town, but to the adjacent area of Bassetlaw, where the Duke of Newcastle enjoyed unchallenged, old-style electoral influence, the Huskissonites resigned. Wellington made no attempt to stop them, though he would miss their debating talents in the House of Commons.

By one of those tortuous links which history so often traces, the Huskissonite resignations precipitated a much more serious Tory split. The president of the Board of Trade, Charles Grant, resigned with Huskisson in May 1828. His successor, William Vesey Fitzgerald, the son of an Irish peer, represented County Clare in the Commons. By a practice not finally abolished until 1926, any MP accepting government office had to resign his seat and submit himself for re-election. In normal circumstances a new minister was either returned unopposed or easily won the resulting by-election. But a movement for Catholic civil rights had been gathering momentum in Ireland during the 1820s, orchestrated by the Catholic Association, whose leader was Daniel O'Connell. O'Connell decided to oppose Fitzgerald, both as an expression of opposition to Wellington's anti-Catholic government and as a means of showing to the British the strength of Irish feelings.

O'Connell duly won a by-election rich in propaganda on both sides. The Catholics, many of whom qualified as forty-shilling freeholders though their property holdings were extremely small, voted in large numbers and the result presented the British government with an acute dilemma. O'Connell had been elected, but under existing legislation could not take his seat since he was a Catholic. If the government refused to change the law, the Catholic Association would instigate immense popular agitation. Civil unrest, including the refusal to pay rent to 'alien' English landlords or tithes to the Anglican church, was all too likely. But concessions in Ireland would be seen by Wellington's staunchest supporters as a betrayal of their most dearly held principles. Almost by choice, Wellington had got rid of the 'liberal' Tories; he could scarcely survive a revolt by the Tory right wing. These 'Ultra-Tories', as they became known, were an important force.

When Wellington and his henchman Peel opted for peac[e]
Ireland by granting Roman Catholic emancipation in 1829,
expected split materialized. The 'Ultras' were not appeased by
government's raising the Irish voting qualification to 10 pou[nds]
to exclude the dangerous Catholic peasantry. Wellington and P[eel]
were branded traitors. The conservative alliance which had rul[ed]
Britain since the 1790s finally came to an end. Wellington, wh[o]
thought himself above any squalid party battles, now found himself leading a smaller, demoralized Tory faction whose contro[l]
over parliament was slipping away.

Catholic emancipation not only detached the 'Ultras' from the
government; it even converted a few of them to parliamentary
reform. Though their position may seem perverse it was not
illogical. They pointed out that only government control of the
rotten boroughs had secured a majority for emancipation. The
measure had little real popular support. If the people could be consulted, the argument ran, they would rally to the cry of 'No
Popery'. The Englishman's dislike of foreigners was legendary
and the Irish were not only foreigners, they were Catholic
foreigners. So, a wider franchise should secure a parliament which
would repeal the Emancipation Act.

Thus it was that the first Reform Bill of the crisis came to be
proposed not by a radical leader, not by Lord John Russell, but by
an Ultra-Tory, the Marquis of Blandford. In February 1830, he
proposed the abolition of all rotten boroughs and their transfer to
the counties and large towns, a maximum parliamentary life of
five years, payment for MPs, a householder franchise in the
boroughs and an extension of the county franchise to include
copyholders, who held land by custom without formally owning
it. It was defeated by 160 votes to 57. Without coming near to
success, Russell got more votes for the much more modest
proposal to enfranchise Birmingham, Manchester and Leeds and
to set an agreed householder qualification in the boroughs. The
recent turmoil in the Tory party had greatly improved Whig
morale and a workable pro-reform alliance between Whigs and
Radicals was being forged.

While events at Westminster were weakening the anti-
reformers, the real pressure for reform was building up outside.

disturb the tranquillity of Eu[rope]
uneasy reminder of the event[s]

Before parliament had t[he]
labourers in Kent, weakened
and a shortage of jobs, had b[een]
outbreaks (the 'Swing Riots')
to December 1831. Some la[bouring]
workers, normally the most
of men, were taking the law
fabric of society was at risk.
in the 1790s and as late as 18
and order could be preserve[d]
some well-publicized treaso[n]
that a similar remedy in 18
lion. MPs therefore began
Was the granting of parlia[mentary]
revolution?

Even the old electoral s[ystem]
strength of feeling outside
in June necessitated a gene[ral]
Wellington's governmen[t]
his majority at a stroke –
Too few contests took p[lace]
complexion likely, and
boroughs and in Scotla[nd]
general elections had str
last important election,
minister, Pitt, a parliam
lacked. Wellington lo[oked]
improve his position, b[ut]
to unseat members of t[he]
party failed dismally.
government patronage
government supporter[s]
brother Jonathan, wer[e]
larger constituencies,
be against reform wer[e]
reformers such as Th[e]

26

and East Retford (Nottinghamshire) and to reallocate their seats to Manchester and Birmingham. When Peel proposed a government amendment which would have given the East Retford seats not to a large manufacturing town, but to the adjacent area of Bassetlaw, where the Duke of Newcastle enjoyed unchallenged, old-style electoral influence, the Huskissonites resigned. Wellington made no attempt to stop them, though he would miss their debating talents in the House of Commons.

By one of those tortuous links which history so often traces, the Huskissonite resignations precipitated a much more serious Tory split. The president of the Board of Trade, Charles Grant, resigned with Huskisson in May 1828. His successor, William Vesey Fitzgerald, the son of an Irish peer, represented County Clare in the Commons. By a practice not finally abolished until 1926, any MP accepting government office had to resign his seat and submit himself for re-election. In normal circumstances a new minister was either returned unopposed or easily won the resulting by-election. But a movement for Catholic civil rights had been gathering momentum in Ireland during the 1820s, orchestrated by the Catholic Association, whose leader was Daniel O'Connell. O'Connell decided to oppose Fitzgerald, both as an expression of opposition to Wellington's anti-Catholic government and as a means of showing to the British the strength of Irish feelings.

O'Connell duly won a by-election rich in propaganda on both sides. The Catholics, many of whom qualified as forty-shilling freeholders though their property holdings were extremely small, voted in large numbers and the result presented the British government with an acute dilemma. O'Connell had been elected, but under existing legislation could not take his seat since he was a Catholic. If the government refused to change the law, the Catholic Association would instigate immense popular agitation. Civil unrest, including the refusal to pay rent to 'alien' English landlords or tithes to the Anglican church, was all too likely. But concessions in Ireland would be seen by Wellington's staunchest supporters as a betrayal of their most dearly held principles. Almost by choice, Wellington had got rid of the 'liberal' Tories; he could scarcely survive a revolt by the Tory right wing. These 'Ultra-Tories', as they became known, were an important force.

When Wellington and his henchman Peel opted for peace in Ireland by granting Roman Catholic emancipation in 1829, the expected split materialized. The 'Ultras' were not appeased by the government's raising the Irish voting qualification to 10 pounds to exclude the dangerous Catholic peasantry. Wellington and Peel were branded traitors. The conservative alliance which had ruled Britain since the 1790s finally came to an end. Wellington, who thought himself above any squalid party battles, now found himself leading a smaller, demoralized Tory faction whose control over parliament was slipping away.

Catholic emancipation not only detached the 'Ultras' from the government; it even converted a few of them to parliamentary reform. Though their position may seem perverse it was not illogical. They pointed out that only government control of the rotten boroughs had secured a majority for emancipation. The measure had little real popular support. If the people could be consulted, the argument ran, they would rally to the cry of 'No Popery'. The Englishman's dislike of foreigners was legendary and the Irish were not only foreigners, they were Catholic foreigners. So, a wider franchise should secure a parliament which would repeal the Emancipation Act.

Thus it was that the first Reform Bill of the crisis came to be proposed not by a radical leader, not by Lord John Russell, but by an Ultra-Tory, the Marquis of Blandford. In February 1830, he proposed the abolition of all rotten boroughs and their transfer to the counties and large towns, a maximum parliamentary life of five years, payment for MPs, a householder franchise in the boroughs and an extension of the county franchise to include copyholders, who held land by custom without formally owning it. It was defeated by 160 votes to 57. Without coming near to success, Russell got more votes for the much more modest proposal to enfranchise Birmingham, Manchester and Leeds and to set an agreed householder qualification in the boroughs. The recent turmoil in the Tory party had greatly improved Whig morale and a workable pro-reform alliance between Whigs and Radicals was being forged.

While events at Westminster were weakening the anti-reformers, the real pressure for reform was building up outside

As ever, economic distress promoted political causes. The 1829 harvest failed, pushing up food prices. At the same time unemployment was on the increase in the cities. William Cobbett, the veteran reformer, who had defied anyone 'to agitate a fellow on a full stomach', saw that bellies were emptying. He returned to his pungent blend of journalistic rhetoric, reminding his readers, as he had told them in 1816, that the real cause of the people's distress was misgovernment. A landowners' parliament was wasting the nation's taxes on lavish expenditure, patronage and corruption.

The alliance between middle classes and working classes, essential for the success of any extra-parliamentary campaign, was much more extensively developed between 1829 and 1832 than ever before. In January 1830 the radical Birmingham banker, Thomas Attwood, formed a 'General Political Union between the Lower and the Middle classes of the people' in that city. Its purpose was to agitate for reform. During 1830, the Birmingham example was followed in most other cities, despite the obvious economic differences which separated millowners and workforces in south Lancashire and the West Riding of Yorkshire. The precise objectives of many unions were deliberately fudged, since working-class leaders naturally favoured full male suffrage while their middle-class allies still distrusted democracy. But, for the moment, the fact of a workable alliance proved more important than the disagreements over strategy. In 1830 and 1831 the political unions were able to assemble a powerful engine of non-violent agitation: political rallies, demonstrations and a fusillade of reform petitions. As an anti-Aristocratic movement especially strong in the unprecedentedly influential industrial areas of Britain, it dwarfed anything hitherto seen.

These developments were greeted with increasing nervousness at Westminster. Politicians had long recognized the growing importance of the middle classes. The working classes on their own, they judged, could still be defied, but in alliance with the middle classes they were unstoppable. Nervousness gave way to alarm in July 1830 when a rebellion in Paris overthrew the anti-reformist French king, Charles x, installed Louis Philippe and initiated a programme of reforms which briefly threatened to disturb the tranquillity of Europe. The July Revolution was an uneasy reminder of the events of 1789.

Before parliament had time to draw breath, agricultural labourers in Kent, weakened and demoralized by harvest failures and a shortage of jobs, had begun to burn hayricks in a series of outbreaks (the 'Swing Riots') which continued from August 1830 to December 1831. Some landowners feared that if agricultural workers, normally the most docile and least politically conscious of men, were taking the law into their own hands then the entire fabric of society was at risk. The problem now was that, whereas in the 1790s and as late as 1819, MPs had rightly believed that law and order could be preserved by a series of repressive statutes and some well-publicized treason trials, evidence was now mounting that a similar remedy in 1830–1 might spark off a full scale rebellion. MPs therefore began seriously to contemplate concessions. Was the granting of parliamentary reform the only way to avoid revolution?

Even the old electoral system provided evidence in 1830 of the strength of feeling outside Westminster. The death of George IV in June necessitated a general election, which perceptibly weakened Wellington's government. It was not that the election destroyed his majority at a stroke – unreformed elections were not like that. Too few contests took place to make a total change in political complexion likely, and government influence in many Cornish boroughs and in Scotland remained strong. Yet, traditionally, general elections had strengthened the government's hand. The last important election, that of 1784, had given the new prime minister, Pitt, a parliamentary majority which he had previously lacked. Wellington looked similarly to the 1830 election to improve his position, but he was sorely disappointed. An attempt to unseat members of the Canning-Huskisson wing of the Tory party failed dismally. Party managers ruefully recognized that government patronage no longer carried its old weight. Notable government supporters, such as John Wilson Croker and Peel's brother Jonathan, were defeated. Where contests were held in the larger constituencies, those brave enough to declare themselves to be against reform were resoundingly beaten. Long standing anti-reformers such as Thomas Gooch, a Suffolk MP since 1806 and

E. P. Bastard, whose family had held one of the two Devon county seats without a break since 1784 were beaten. Most spectacularly, a reforming Whig with a non-aristocratic background, Henry Brougham, took on and beat the Whig establishment in Yorkshire, though he had no previous connections with a county renowned for its antipathy to outsiders.

Reform was the central issue of the 1830 election. Lord Wharncliffe expressed his opinion to Wellington a little later: 'The demonstration in favour of Reform at the general election of 1830 satisfied me that the feeling upon it was not . . . temporary and likely to die away.' The election had three critical effects. It gravely weakened Wellington's government. It demonstrated the vote-winning possibilities of reform even among the restricted pre-1832 electorate. And it convinced remaining Whig doubters that support for reform was their best prospect of a return to power after a generation of opposition.

The election took place in July and August. Wellington's administration staggered on, demoralized and rudderless, until parliament reassembled in November. In the meantime popular agitation had increased in intensity. Southern and eastern hayricks continued to be burnt; radicals in the north and midlands used the example of France to advance the cause of democracy; the situation was further complicated by industrial unrest among Lancashire cotton spinners and South Wales miners during October.

In November 1830 Wellington, taunted by Grey's homilies that concessions on reform were the only route to political salvation, made his famous, ill-fated response. The Lords were solemnly told that the prime minister

> was fully convinced that the country possessed at the present moment a legislature which answered all the good purposes of legislation, and this to a greater degree than any legislature ever had answered in any country whatever. He would go further and say that the legislature and the system of representation possessed the full and entire confidence of the country.

Wellington, having bent on Catholic Emancipation to his great personal embarrassment, remained ramrod straight against political reform.

This spectacular piece of political misjudgment had precisely the opposite consequence of that intended. Wellington had hoped to stiffen the resolve of his supporters; instead he made them more fearful of the effects of continued resistance. The Huskissonite Tories made common cause with the Whigs and the fall of the government was now assured. It occurred on no great issue, but on a minor financial matter only a fortnight after Wellington's outburst. His ministers, in general, were glad to relinquish the burdens of office.

No alternative Tory administration was available to the new king, William IV. So Earl Grey, who as Charles Grey had been ridiculed for pressing the reform issue onto a hostile parliament in 1793, became prime minister thirty-seven years later in a Whig government pledged to parliamentary reform. It would be wrong to suggest that Grey had maintained an unswerving commitment to parliamentary reform during the long intervening period, but the reform which his government now sought to pilot through parliament bore striking resemblances to the proposals of the Friends of the People (see pp. 14–16).

A ministerial committee under Lord Durham wrestled with complexities of contending reform proposals during the winter of 1830–1. Lord John Russell, by now a veteran in such matters, was charged with the task of presenting a bill for which there was at last a prospect of success. Grey's aims underlay the specific proposals: the measure must be 'large enough to satisfy public opinion and to afford sure ground of resistance to further innovation'. No one should expect the Whigs to be democrats; they were aristocratic, and Grey's Cabinet of 1830 was one of the most blue-blooded in the nineteenth century. Grey realized, however, that mere tinkering with the existing system would not satisfy the much-heightened public expectation.

In January 1831 Durham's committee proposed to the Cabinet a scheme which was a curious mixture of the bold and the timid. Most surprisingly, it recommended a secret ballot, but proposed to reduce the effects of such audacity by establishing a standard qualification for a borough vote at the forbiddingly high level of property worth at least £20 a year. Such a provision would have reduced many existing electorates substantially; Bristol's, for example, would have been cut by about a half. More predictably, Durham proposed to disfranchise 61 boroughs entirely and to remove one of the two members from 47 more. Most of the seats would go to the counties and industrial towns, but the opportunity would be taken to reduce the size of the Commons from 658 members to 596.

These proposals were not submitted to public debate. The Cabinet would have nothing to do with a secret ballot but, under Grey's perceptive guidance, they agreed to substitute a £10 household franchise for the £20 one. Grey was convinced that public opinion would tolerate no higher threshold and it was a substantial hurdle. Nor was the proposal to compensate dispossessed borough owners for their loss considered tactful in a reforming administration. So, some hasty re-drafting of the Durham committee recommendations was necessary before Russell could present the government's proposals to the Commons in March 1831. They caused an outcry. MPs, by now well used to Russell's proposals to disfranchise a few rotten boroughs, were amazed at their radicalism. Outside parliament the general reaction was one of relief that a government had at last grasped the nettle. Attwood was confident that the proposals would not endanger his newly forged alliance between the middle and working classes. Many working-class leaders were temporarily dazzled by proposals for a uniform franchise. Only Henry Hetherington, editor of a new publication, *Poor Man's Guardian* whose central campaigning platform was one man one vote, saw the real implications of the £10 borough franchise. It would give the vote to small shopkeepers and tradesmen whilst withholding it from most working men. He was perceptive enough to appreciate that few sectors of society were more hostile to working-class political representation than the lower middle classes, on the well-established principle that those one rung further up any ladder are the most fearful of clamouring feet immediately below. Thus, while Bronterre O'Brien and John Doherty urged working people to support the bill as a necessary first instalment to the reform from which they would directly benefit, Hetherington counselled opposition on the grounds that it would be used not to foster but to block more radical change.

Debates in parliament fired ancient passions. Macaulay made a most persuasive contribution, arguing the necessity to adhere the middle classes firmly to the existing constitution by including them in it. Opponents of reform either, like J. W. Croker, pointed out anomalies in the proposed scheme or, like Sir Robert Inglis or Robert Peel, concentrated on the dangers of novelty and on the tried and tested virtues of the existing system. Peel in 1831 echoed Pitt in 1793: 'Let us never be tempted to resign the well tempered freedom which we enjoy, in the ridiculous pursuit of the wild liberty which France has established . . . liberty which has neither justice nor wisdom for its companions.'

Grey was dismayed by the tenacity of his opponents. His bill passed its second reading stage by a single vote (302 to 301) on 22 March in the biggest parliamentary division ever recorded. Such a narrow victory, far less than had been predicted, was quite insufficient to guard against damaging amendments as the bill trundled through discussion in committee. In a wider context, however, Grey could draw comfort from the composition of his victory. County members voted for the reform by a majority of two to one; borough members whose seats would remain after 1832 voted for it in almost an equal proportion; the Irish supported it by about three to two proportionally. An appeal to the electorate would stand an excellent chance of strengthening his hand.

So, when the first adverse amendment was carried in committee, Grey persuaded a most reluctant William IV to break with convention and dissolve parliament after less than a year. The elections of April/May 1831 were a huge triumph for the reformers. They won almost all the 'open' boroughs. Only six of the thirty-four county MPs who had voted against reform either on second reading or in the critical amendment got back to parliament. Grey had a majority in excess of 130 seats in the Commons after an election which became virtually a plebiscite on reform.

But the Commons was not synonymous with Parliament. In the House of Lords an intractable anti-reform majority remained, unelected and apparently immovable. It is an interesting commentary on radical reformers that they paid little attention to the House of Lords, believing with Paine that the Lords would wither away once reform of the lower house was accomplished.

The events of the next few months showed what an obstacle the Lords could be. If reform were to be carried 'by due process of law', then that process necessitated majorities in both houses of parliament. The Lords could exercise an absolute veto on even the largest Commons majority.

A large Commons majority was not long in coming. In July 1831 a second reform bill, very similar to the first, passed through the Commons with a majority of almost 140. The committee stage involved some intricate horse trading in which some boroughs were given reprieves and other new towns enfranchised. The only important change was that introduced by Lord Chandos, who carried an amendment to enfranchise county tenants renting property worth at least £50 a year. The change could be justified on grounds of providing an extension of county voters parallel with that provided for the boroughs but, as we shall see (p. 38) it had important political implications.

The bill arrived in the Lords on 22 September 1831. In the early hours of 8 October, after a fiery debate, they threw it out by a majority of 41. Later that same day, riots broke out in Derby and Nottingham and during the rest of the month extensive rioting was experienced both in large towns, most notably Bristol, and in small ones like the west of England woollen towns, Blandford and Tiverton. In towns which did not riot, new political unions were formed or existing ones strengthened; mass meetings and processions were held; vitriolic anti-aristocratic resolutions were passed with acclamation. Hostility was directed also against the hierarchy of the Church of England since of twenty-six bishops who sat in the Lords, twenty-one had voted with the majority. Had they voted otherwise, a reform act would have been passed in 1831.

Britain has never in modern times been closer to revolution than in the autumn of 1831. Cabinet members seriously doubted whether the archaic system of national defence could withstand the strains now put upon it. With the partial exception of London, after Peel's experiment in 1829, no police force yet existed. The army was neither large enough nor trained enough to cope with widespread rioting. At his country seat, Drayton Manor, Peel laid in quantities of arms to withstand a possible seige by Staffordshire rioters. Possibly, only the government's professed determination to continue with reform prevented a grand explosion.

The riots, in addition to thoroughly alarming the authorities, did emphasize one standing weakness of the extra-parliamentary reformers, namely that the middle classes did not riot in October 1831. Indeed, many small shopkeepers feared for their own property and, at least temporarily, placed a higher priority on law and order than they did on reform. The latent hostility between middle classes and working classes surfaced. Thomas Attwood, seeing the danger, helped to keep the reform forces more or less together with an ambiguous call to the middle classes to arm themselves. While Grey and the Whigs could take this as further evidence of the pro-reform determination of the middle classes, many small tradesmen were only too happy to obey Attwood's call — but to defend themselves against 'the rabble'.

The Whigs meanwhile sought ways of overthrowing the anti-reform majority in the Lords. When Russell presented the third reform bill to the Commons in December, substantial changes had been made to the list of boroughs scheduled to lose one of their two members. These were reduced in number from 41 to 30 and ten proposed new boroughs were now given not one member, but two. The Commons majority, unimportantly, moved up to 162. The battle was to take place in the Lords. Many ministers, led by Durham, were convinced that the constitutional *impasse* could be resolved only by the creation of sufficient new peers known to favour reform to outvote the anti-reformers. But William IV, who regarded such a manoeuvre as both a constitutional and a social outrage, would have to be coerced. Grey counselled caution, urging that the mere threat to dilute blue blood to a turquoise rinse would be enough. For the moment, ministers left matters as they were, and were rewarded in April 1832 with a Lords majority of nine in favour of the new bill. Further consultations followed with opposition leaders in the hope of avoiding defeats in committee. Grey was even prepared to reprieve more boroughs and restrict the number of new industrial seats, but to no avail. A wrecking amendment was carried in the first week of May. Grey rushed to the King to demand fifty new peers immediately. The King refused to be hurried: Grey tendered his resignation.

So began the crisis known as the 'Days of May'. William IV asked Wellington to investigate the possibility of forming a ministry which would promote a more modest reform bill. Wellington, as opposed to reform as ever, but finally appreciating that in some form it must come, agreed to try. Predominantly Tory peers might be persuaded to pass a Tory reform measure when they had been reluctant to pass a Whig one.

Extra-parliamentary hostility, which had provoked the Reform Crisis, now had a further say in determining its outcome. Thomas Attwood and Francis Place, 'the radical tailor of Charing Cross' who had enjoyed a long career of reforming political manipulation beginning with the London Corresponding Society in the 1790s, organized yet more demonstrations, now of hostility to Wellington. Westminster was flooded with anti-Tory petitions. Forms of middle-class coercion were canvassed. Property owners should withhold taxes. More subtly, Place suggested that investors should all withdraw their assets from the banks at once, precipitating a financial on top of a political crisis: 'To stop the Duke', ran the slogan, 'go for Gold'. Loose talk of armed resistance was bandied about, though the nation as a whole was less frenzied than in the previous October and Wellington's ability to form a government had yet to be tested.

In the event, he failed since his old ally, Peel, refused to join any government pledged to reform. A Tory government without Peel would have had no chance of success and Peel, though not a last-ditch opponent of reform, felt compromised by his actions on the Catholic question in 1829. He had deserted the anti-reform Tories once; to do it again, he calculated, would finish his career. Once Peel had refused to serve, Wellington informed the King that he was unable to form a government. Four tortured days later, William swallowed his pride and asked Grey, whose tendered resignation he had not formally accepted, to take again the reins of government with the critical promise that he would, when necessary, create sufficient peers to bludgeon the Lords into submission.

The need for extra peers never came. Parliamentary opposition collapsed once Wellington confessed defeat. Most of the peers who had frustrated Grey in May absented themselves from the upper house when, on 4 June, the third reading of the third reform bill was passed by 106 votes to 22. Popular agitation was quietened. Perhaps fortunately for them, Place and Attwood had no need to make good their threats of civil disruption. We can never know what would have happened if the Lords had called the radicals' bluff and kept to their anti-reforming principles. Nothing is more certain, however, than that reform was peacefully enacted in June 1832 not because noble lords were persuaded by the merits of the case, but because they feared the consequences of continued resistance.

What did the Reform Act of 1832 change, and in whose interest?

In this section, frequent reference is made to the specific changes brought about by the Reform Act. These are itemized in the Appendices, which should be consulted alongside the text.

Evaluation of the first Reform Act has been hampered by two opposing oversimplifications. It used to be assumed that the Act was responsible for making the middle classes the rulers of Britain. In 1832, they entered the political kingdom, in appropriate recognition of their industrial and commercial might. But the middle classes were no more the rulers of Britain in, say, 1860 than they had been in 1830. Appreciation of this fact has led to an equally misleading myth – that the Reform Act was a measure of relatively little significance, whose importance was grotesquely exaggerated by contemporaries both inside parliament and in the nation at large. The introduction to this essay attempts briefly to argue the fallacy of that view.

The precise terms of the Act, particularly the lists of boroughs disfranchised, was the result of compromises made at the height of the crisis of 1831–2. The general strategy of reform, however, was clear enough and the 1832 Act did not betray it. Grey told the Lords in 1831 that 'The principle of my reform is, to prevent the necessity for revolution . . . there is no one more dedicated against annual parliaments, universal suffrage, and the ballot, than I am.' This was no window dressing by a politician anxious to extract votes from a hostile audience. Grey believed in 1831, as in 1793, that moderate reform was the only secure route to political stability. He would not abandon the principle of aristocratic government; rather the Whigs would strengthen it by attaching to the existing constitution the new forms of propertied interest. What Grey and the Whigs wished to preserve above all things was the continuance of government by men of property. Absolutely no contradiction existed between the preservation of property rights and a considerable extension of the franchise.

The Whigs aimed to frustrate democracy by increasing the franchise. The paradox in this is only superficial. Those who were enfranchised for the first time in 1832 were, overwhelmingly, small property owners, a numerically significant proportion of the population. Appendix 2 indicates how significant the increase in the number of voters was. After 1832, about one adult male in five was entitled to vote in England and Wales, compared with just over one in ten before. In Scotland the prospect of real elections existed for the first time after 1832, though only one male in eight had the vote. Ireland, of course, had a more restricted county electorate (Appendix 1c) since it was deemed unwise to enfranchise large numbers of Catholic peasants. Only five per cent of Irishmen were entitled to vote after 1832. It is interesting to notice the increased numbers of men entitled to vote between the first Reform Act and the second, because of increased prosperity and gentle inflation rather than further changes in electoral law, was almost exactly matched by the rise in population; the proportion of voters in the population as a whole hardly changed (Appendix 2).

The purpose of a uniform £10 borough qualification (Appendix 1) was twofold. It kept out non-property owners, who were deemed unworthy to be trusted with the vote, and it made a move to replace the chaos of borough franchises which had been so evident before 1832. The precise effects of the change differed markedly across the country since rental values varied. In London, where they were high, many skilled workers with permanent residences qualified; in Cornwall and parts of Wales, where they were very low, even some shopkeepers were kept off the voting roll. In the midland and northern towns, on whose representation so much discussion had centred, the qualification was intentionally stiff. In Leeds, for example, a city of some 125,000 people in 1831 a high proportion of whom were industrial workers, only 5,000 people were entitled to vote in 1832. Birmingham had approximately 7,000 houses worth £10 a year in a total population of 144,000 and Manchester about 13,000 in a population of 182,000. In some constituencies, such as Preston, Coventry and Westminster where the pre-1832 franchise had been unusually wide, the proportion actually declined once old voters began to die. Lancaster's electors dwindled from about 4,000 in 1832 to about 1,000 over the next generation.

In the counties, much controversy attended the passage of the Chandos amendment which enfranchised tenants. The amendment increased the county electorate by about 30 per cent more than the Whigs intended and it was contentious because it was feared that a move, superficially in the direction of greater representation, would actually increase the influence of the aristocracy. Since 1832 brought no secret ballot (Appendix 4), it was feared that landlords would tell tenants whom to vote for, on pain of eviction when their leases expired. The possibilities of influence undoubtedly existed. Landlords could also increase forty-shilling freeholds to enable more people to vote on their behalf. But such methods proved only minor factors in the continued influence of landowners over the political system. Landowners and their agents were men of business and agriculture had become a highly profit-conscious enterprise. Proprietors would lose more than they would gain by evicting politically hostile tenants for the sake of a few extra votes if those tenants were good farmers. It was true, however, that most of these new county voters were of the same political persuasion as their landlords. After 1832, farmers were overwhelmingly Tory.

The registration of voters (Appendix 1) had extremely important political consequences. After 1832, it was not enough for a potential elector to satisfy the property qualification; he must get himself onto the electoral register. The number of houses rated at £10 or more is not always a reliable guide to the number of electors since, in the nineteenth century as in the twentieth, by no means all potential voters expressed enthusiasm for the political process. The emergence of the local party agent was the natural consequence. Good agents proved themselves worth their weight in gold. They tramped the streets ascertaining where support lay among prospective voters and then guided those voters through the sometimes complex registration process in the Revising Barrister's Court.

Obviously, it was to a party's advantage to get as many of its own supporters onto the register as possible and, by arguing cases in the Revising Courts, to deny as many opponents as could be managed. In the early years after 1832 it was the Tory party which the better manipulated what Peel rightly called 'a perfectly new element of political power'. Professional agents were appointed in most of the large towns and became the vanguard of modern party political organization. The Tories won a famous election victory in 1841 and, though many textbooks have concentrated on Whig shortcomings in office, at least as much attention should be paid to the efficiency of Tory party organization in the boroughs. When both parties were well organized in the 1860s, the new registration system permitted a realistic assessment to be made of the numbers entitled to vote. In the 1830s and 1840s the composition of a borough list often tells more about the strength of the respective party organizations. Since many dead men 'voted' in the early years while others were prevented from doing so by various subterfuges at which agents rapidly became adept, it might be said that the Reform Act actually added new potential for manipulation.

The old means of corruption were not eliminated in 1832. Bribing and treating of voters continued. A committee under the Marquis of Hartington reported in 1870 (after the passage of the *second* Reform Act) that 'a considerable class of voters will not vote unless they are paid'. Lancaster, St Albans and Totnes all had reputations for notorious corruption. Rioting and revelling at election times was not unknown in Victorian England. Indeed, since more contests took place after 1832 opportunities for corruption may even have increased. Between 1784 and 1831 roughly 30 per cent of seats were actually contested; in the elections between the first and second Reform Acts, $52\frac{1}{2}$ per cent of seats went to the polls.

The lack of legislation to eliminate electoral 'influence' after 1832 (Appendix 4) is quite deliberate. Any move towards 'fairer' elections or equal electoral districts could be interrupted as a dangerous compromise with the principles of democracy. In preparing the list of enfranchised and disfranchised boroughs, Russell was careful to inform the Commons in 1831, the government 'had never put the measure of Reform on a footing of such perfect symmetry and regularity as to reduce the Representation of the country to exact proportions . . . anomalies they found, and anomalies, though not such glaring ones as now existed, they meant to leave'. So boroughs like Thetford, Reigate, Westbury and Calne survived in 1832 although none had more than 200 voters. Croydon, Doncaster and Loughborough had populations in excess of 10,000 in 1831, but were not dignified with a parliamentary seat. County representation in England was increased by 59 seats, but the counties were still numerically under-represented with 57 per cent of the electorate, but only 32 per cent of the seats.

'Managed' or 'pocket' boroughs also survived, though in reduced numbers. Professor Gash estimates that between 60 and 70 MPs continued to fill parliamentary seats because of patronage. Pocket boroughs did have some intrinsic merit. They did allow able, but inevitably well connected, men to enter parliament very young and thus to build long careers in the service of the nation: the parliaments after 1832 still had a large proportion of men in their twenties. No less than 36 per cent of members of the Commons of 1841–7 had been first elected before they reached their thirtieth birthdays. One of these was William Ewart Gladstone, who came from a very prosperous commercial family in Liverpool: he had been recommended to the Duke of Newcastle as a likely young man and firm in the Tory interest. The Duke presented him to the borough of Newark in Nottinghamshire whose electors duly returned him to the first reformed parliament in December 1832; Gladstone was just short of 23 years old. Gladstone's immensely long parliamentary career, most of it subsequently in the Liberal party, began in the new House in exactly the same way as had those of Pitt the Younger and Charles James Fox in the old: selected for a pocket borough almost as soon as he came of age.

Continuity after 1832 went much further than the survival of a reduced number of managed boroughs. Effectively, the same people ruled Britain. Of those elected in December 1832, between 70 and 80 per cent represented the landed interest; the largest specific category was that comprising the sons of the peerage. Not more than one hundred members were bankers, merchants or manufacturers. Many pre-1832 parliaments had returned similar numbers of the professional and industrial middle classes. Althorp's prediction in December 1831 that MPs 'would continue to be selected from the same classes as at present' proved accurate enough. Though the middle classes had the vote, they did not return a significantly larger number of middle class MPs. A slow change set in from the 1840s but at least until the 1870s parliament remained in overall aristocratic control. Neither were radical MPs more numerous. Only 46 MPs could be persuaded by Attwood in July 1839 to vote even for consideration of the Chartist petition for universal manhood suffrage and five other democratic demands. Democracy continued to be a dirty word in the reformed Commons.

Why were the rising middle classes so poorly represented? The reasons are partly practical and partly psychological. Many businessmen were intensely interested in politics, but they found local questions far more rewarding. Between the 1830s and the 1860s much more attention was given in places like Leeds and Birmingham to issues such as local public health, education and civic amenities than to national politics. Local elections were contested with an intensity which late-twentieth-century voters, generally too bored with them to vote at all, would find astounding. The Victorian city, however, symbolized modern civilization and its governance was a matter of first importance. Civic pride motivated men for whom parliament was remote not only geographically, but also to their immediate concerns. It should not be forgotten that mid-nineteenth-century governments exercised far less influence over local affairs than do the governments of today.

Local communities retained much autonomy, but the government of an increasingly complex industrial society still required more parliamentary time than hitherto. Parliamentary sessions lengthened and, for the first time, MPs could choose to interpret

41

their jobs as full-time ones. Since parliamentary duties remained unpaid (Appendix 4) only MPs of private means, or able to make money in London at times convenient for parliamentary sittings, such as lawyers and bankers, could afford the financial sacrifice required. Most men of private means had inherited wealth and most inherited wealth was landed in origin. A cotton manufacturer, unless his business was well established or his faith in his business partners total, needed to be near his mills. The landowner, and still more his sons, could leave day-to-day administration in the hands of agents. It is not surprising that parliament was still dominated by gentlemen of leisure.

The psychological reasons for the continuing landed dominance of parliament may be the most important of all. There is little evidence to suggest that the middle classes were avid to grasp political power. They demanded representation, taking the view that the vote was more valuable as a privilege to be won than as a 'right of man' to be demanded. Fundamentally, most were as conservative as their social superiors. As Michael Brock puts it, 'most of the new voters wanted not to challenge the aristocracy, but to win recognition from it: once they had their rightful position they did not favour further adventures'. It is one of the less endearing foibles of human nature that most people can find reasons to attack clubs of which they are not members. Once admitted to any privileged circle, they can find good cause for defending the very institutions they once derided. As Grey had calculated, the middle classes soon proved themselves a reassuringly conservative force. Some of the most devastating attacks on the Chartist democrats of the 1830s and 1840s came from those small shopkeepers and tradesmen who ten years earlier had made common cause with working men to alarm the establishment into political reform.

The doom-laden prophecies of the Tory opponents of reform, therefore, proved ludicrously wide of the mark. J. W. Croker had said that 'The reform Bill is a stepping stone in England to a republic. The Bill once passed, goodnight to the Monarchy, and the Lords and the Church.' Yet we still wait, with no obvious signs of impatience, to bid adieu to any of them. Wellington expected that 'we shall be destroyed one after the other . . . by

42

due course of law.' The old soldier lived for twenty years after the passage of the Reform Act, most of them spent still at the centre of politics. Had he been much given either to reflection or introspection he would have recognized the folly of this utterance long before his death.

What Grey and his colleagues had done was to forge the most durable of political alliances, that between land and industry; it would stand fast for many years against the assaults of the democrats. It is no wonder that working-class leaders spoke so bitterly about their old allies, the middle classes, after 1832. The rights of property had been given a new lease of life, largely under existing management. Britain, alone of the advanced nations of western Europe, avoided political revolution in the 1830s and 1840s. Those revolutions depended to a significant extent upon middle-class leadership. The middle classes in Britain had been hitched to the waggon of established authority. In the short term, the Reform Act strengthened the *status quo*.

But in the longer term, of course, the Reform Act opened the door to more dramatic changes, as Peel had feared it would. The 1832 Act could not be, as Lord John Russell had presented it, 'the final solution of a great constitutional question'. By 1848, Russell himself was convinced that a new dose of reform was necessary. Within thirty years, politicians recognized that they would have to trust working men with the vote. By the end of the century, it would not be a misnomer to talk of a middle-class dominated parliament. Soon enough, the aristocracy would have to share an influence which they had been used to exercising alone. But it would be a sharing of powers, however unequally and uneasily, not the crude supersession of one ruling class by another. This is the true measure of the 1832 Reform Act. For all its imperfections, it set a modern industrial state firmly on the path to gradual, non-violent change. That is why it deserves to be remembered as the pre-eminent piece of legislation in nineteenth-century Britain.

Select Bibliography

The following brief guide should suffice for those students who wish to be more fully acquainted with the subject.

1 J. Cannon, *Parliamentary Reform, 1640–1832* (2nd ed., Cambridge, 1980).
2 M. Brock, *The Great Reform Act* (London, 1973).
   These are now the standard works and both contain full bibliographies and other scholarly apparatus.
   On Reform before 1789, only briefly surveyed here, see:
3 G. Rude, *Wilkes and Liberty* (Oxford, 1962).
4 I. R. Christie, *Wilkes, Wyvill and Reform* (London, 1962).
   For the reform agitation of the 1790s:
5 A. Goodwin, *The Friends of Liberty* (London, 1979) – a meticulous and authoritative account.
   The distinctive contribution of working people to the agitation for Reform between 1789 and 1832 is brilliantly evoked in
6 E. P. Thompson, *The Making of the English Working Class* (Pelican ed., London, 1968).
   The best study of the political system as it operated immediately after 1832 is
7 N. Gash, *Politics in the Age of Peel* (Revised ed., London, 1977).
   Among textbooks which might profitably be consulted both for specific comments and general background are:
8 I. R. Christie, *Wars and Revolutions, Britain 1760–1815* (London, 1982).
9 N. Gash, *Aristocracy and People, 1815–1865* (London, 1979).
10 E. J. Evans, *The Forging of the Modern State: Early Industrial Britain 1783–1870* (London, 1983).

Appendix 1a
The 1832 Reform Act
(England and Wales)

Qualifications for the vote

IN COUNTY SEATS

i Adult males owning freehold property worth at least 40 shillings (£2) per annum.

ii Adult males in possession of a copyhold worth at least £10 per annum.

iii Adult males leasing or renting land worth at least £50 per annum. (This provision resulted from the 'Chandos Amendment').

IN BOROUGH SEATS

i Adult males owning or occupying property worth at least £10 per annum provided:

  a That they had been in possession of the property for at least one year and had paid all taxes charged on that property.

  b That they had not been in receipt of parish poor relief during the previous year.

ii Voters who did not qualify under i but who had exercised a vote in a borough before 1832 retained the right to vote in that borough (unless, of course, the borough had disappeared under the Act) during their lifetimes, provided that they lived in, or within seven miles of, the borough where they would vote. This right to vote could not be passed on to heirs or successors.

Changes in the distribution of seats

  i 56 borough constituencies (cited as Schedule A boroughs in the Act) lost their representation entirely.

  ii 30 boroughs (Schedule B) lost one of their two members.

  iii 22 new parliamentary boroughs (Schedule C) created with two members.

  iv 19 new parliamentary boroughs (Schedule D) created with one member.

  v County representation increased. One county to have six members; twenty-six to have four members; seven counties to have three members; 6 counties to retain two members; Isle of Wight to become a separate, single-member constituency.

IN WALES

  i In the boroughs the old system of grouping boroughs retained but two new single-member boroughs created.

  ii In the counties, three counties now returned two members; nine counties continued to return one member each.

NB Specific changes itemized in Appendix 2.

Registration

A register of electors to be compiled in each constituency.

Appendix 1b
The 1832 Reform Act (Scotland)

Main qualifications for the franchise

COUNTIES

i All owners of property with a yearly value of at least £10.

ii Leaseholders to the value of £10 if on a lease for life or for not less than fifty-seven years; Leaseholders to the value of £50 on a lease for not less than nineteen years.

iii Tenants of property worth £50.

iv Existing voters, not otherwise qualified, retained the right to vote during their lifetimes.

BURGHS

i All occupiers of property worth at least £10 per annum (same qualification as for England with same caveats on taxes and non-receipt of parochial relief).

ii The old system, whereby town councils elected a delegate who had one vote in election, abolished.

Changes in distribution of seats

COUNTIES

i 30 seats, as before. 27 counties to return one member each. Elgin & Nairn, Ross & Cromarty, Clackmannan and Kinross joined, each group electing one member.

i Representation increased from 15 to 23.

ii Edinburgh and Glasgow to return two members each; Aberdeen, Dundee, Greenock, Paisley and Perth to return one member each.

iii Remaining 14 seats to come from the system, retained from the old practice, of grouping individual boroughs into districts, each of 14 districts to return one member.

Appendix 1c
The 1832 Reform Act (Ireland)

Main qualifications for the franchise

COUNTIES

i All owners of property with a yearly value of at least £10 (NB this was the same provision as had applied since Catholic Emancipation in 1829).

ii Leaseholders to the value of £10 with leases of at least twenty years.

BOROUGHS

i All occupiers of property worth at least £10 per annum (as in England).

ii Some cities were legally considered as 'counties of cities'. Here the right to vote was extended to £10 freeholders and leaseholders.

iii Those entitled to vote before 1832 and not otherwise qualified retained the vote during their lifetime.

Distribution of seats

COUNTIES

Each of the 32 counties returned 2 members, as before.

BOROUGHS AND UNIVERSITY

i To the original 35 borough seats were added one extra member each for Belfast, Galway, Limerick and Waterford.

ii A second seat was given to the University of Dublin with a franchise extending to all holders of M.A. and higher degrees.

49

Appendix 2
Approximate size of the electorate, 1831–66

England and Wales	1831	1833	% Increase 31–33	1866	% Increase 33–66
Counties	201,859	370,379	83	543,633	47
Boroughs	164,391	282,398	71	514,026	82
Combined	366,250	652,777	78	1,056,659	62

Note the large percentage increases in those entitled to vote after the passage of the first Reform Act but before the passage of the second. This was due in part to increased political organization in getting voters onto the new Registers and in part to the effects of modest inflation in bringing more people to the various hurdles for qualification.

Estimated Proportion of Adult Males entitled to vote in England and Wales

1831: 366,250 of 3,463,795 (11%)
1833: 652,777 of 3,577,538 (18%)
1866: 1,056,659 of 5,373,033 (20%)

These are estimates only. The totals of adult males derive from census material and extrapolations of trends between census years.

Appendix 3
The changed composition of the House of Commons

	County Seats 1820*	County Seats 1832	Borough Seats 1820	Borough Seats 1832	University 1820	University 1832	Total 1820	Total 1832
England	80	144	405	323	4	4	489	471
Wales	12	15	12	14	—	—	24	29
Scotland	30	30	15	23	—	—	45	53
Ireland	64	64	35	39	1	2	100	105
Total	186	253	467	399	5	6	658	658

* 1820 was chosen as a convenient pre-reform date since the borough of Grampound was disfranchised in 1821 and its seats transferred to Yorkshire. The Irish members sat in the Commons from 1801, after the passage of the Act of Union.

Appendix 4
Major Radical Items
Not Conceded in 1832

1 No manhood suffrage. Universal male suffrage not achieved until 1918.
2 No annually elected parliaments. Length of parliament remained a maximum of seven years until 1911, when this was reduced to five years.
3 A property qualification for MPs remained. The possession of property to the value of at least £300 a year was a minimum qualification until 1858.
4 No payment of salaries to MPs. MPs remained unpaid until 1911.
5 No secret ballot. Voting remained public until 1872.